RACISM
Understanding The Basics

I0440487

By
Chris Monroe

Find me on Snap Chat, Instagram, Twitter, YouTube and more
@ChrisMonroeSTL

Resale St Louis LLC
2518 Lemay Ferry Rd #101
Saint Louis, MO 63125

CHRISMONROESTL.COM

Contents

About the Author

Chris Monroe also known as Mr. I Stay Woke or the Student Master Teacher is a graduate of Normandy High School class of 2000. He has traveled the world as an active duty supply sergeant in the U.S. Army. He studied paralegal studies and criminal justice in college. He has worked as a club DJ, radio talk show host, public speaker, YouTuber, auctioneer, and even a taxi driver.

After serving overseas in Iraq, he returned to St Louis and was immediately attracted to the resale world. With no jobs available at the time for a hard-working military veteran, he started his own house cleaning business and a consignment business. As a licensed auctioneer and resale professional he has sold thousands of products and services.

In just a few years, he has become a powerful freedom fighter for the liberation of African people. Chris is considered to be a part of the Pan-African movement. He assists in the local community organization Better Family Life in an attempt to uplift, educate and inspire the youth coming up after him.

With his available free time that is left over from running a successful business, he assists others by doing business consultations, product research, development, marketing and sales. With all of these talents, we can expect to see more great things in the future from this great mind.

Find Chris Monroe on ALL social media outlets - @ChrisMonroeSTL

See the main website for more great content - ChrisMonroeSTL.com

Introduction

What's happening, what's happening, what's happening family? It's the Student Master Teacher here, Mr. I Stay Woke; Chris Monroe.   In this book, I break down the basics and fundamentals of racism in America. Many believe that racism is simply name calling and threats to an individual or group. It goes much deeper than you may realize.

Systematic racism is a real problem for minorities in the United States. Learn about the nine areas of battle that African-Americans must compete in to become an independent people. The post-traumatic slavery syndrome still shows it's face on a daily basis in the U.S.

After reading this book, you will see another perspective on how blacks have to take a different posture going forward if the group ever truly wants to see real progress. Discrimination can come from many areas and this book will help you identify racism with examples that you can verify for yourself.

CHRISMONROESTL.COM

The Chris Monroe Show

Monday Night Raw, Radio Style!

7PM Eastern 6 PM Central

Call in 516-418-5565

Part 1
The Basics

Everybody has their own perspective on it but we are going to chop it up into small pieces so that it becomes easy to chew and digest.

I just wanted to break things down into proper perspective on this racism white-supremacy. What is racism? I hear a lot of people saying that, "if a white man calls you a nigger you, then he must be racist." The fact of the matter is that he would be prejudice. Name calling is all it is fueled by hate.

That's part of the problem. We base racism and many other parts of our lives on emotion. We have to stop living inside emotions on everything we do in our lives. We think because somebody calls us a name or call us out of our name that they are a racist. It's deeper than that. Simply because someone hurts our feelings, that in itself does not mean they are a racist person.

Racism-white supremacy goes into multiple areas of life for black people in this country. There are nine basic areas in which must first be aware of and defend these areas of battle. You must understand that the system is like a spider web and it all works together to maintain power and order for the powers that be.

The nine areas of battle are entertainment, education, economics, sex, labor, law, war, politics and last but not least religion. This book will give a brief overview and some examples of each. Remember that one area works hand and hand with other areas to keep us confused and off balance.

Part 2 Entertainment & Media
We all want to be entertained but is it hurting us?

The first area we will discuss is entertainment. This is the news media, the magazines, the movies, the music, you know, everything filled with negativity, destruction and ignorance to show the world that this is what black people are. A good example would be the angry black woman fighting in the streets with a long blonde wig on. Another one is a "thug" dude with the dreadlocks in his hair or what some would call a dread head with the sagging pants and a long white t shirt that looks like a dress on him. All of it is propaganda to paint a picture of who and what black people are. It will always keep your mind programmed to believe that ALL black people are bad and up to no good. According to Dr. Umar Johnson the psychologist, the mind cannot turn off what it sees or what it hears. Therefore, these repeated negative images of black people is deeply rooted in our brain.

Every time you watch the news at night, what do you see? The 10 o'clock news seems to be the same every night.

The first opening story, "Police are searching for this suspect standing about 6 feet tall, 200 pounds, with a tattoo of a tear drop on his face. He has been identified Demarco Johnson and is wanted for armed criminal action" or some name like that and it's a mug shot of a black dude with dreadlocked hair. This is all done to program you and to remind you that crime comes from black folks. Black people equal crime in this country. That's part of the programming and the propaganda that they put on us on a regular basis. So that's why I say it goes deeper than that.

All of the mainstream media seems to promote and produce these negative stereotypical types of news coverage as well as television shows like Empire or Scandal. These shows are widely popular but they always have an underlying theme or agenda hidden in the name of entertainment.

You may be thinking that this is not true. When we think of TV, music and all forms of the media you would think that we as adults should know right from wrong. The problem is that adults are not the only ones watching these types of shows. Children are always watching and learning and that is more of who the media targets. If they can show your child that being gay is socially acceptable or being a black women thirsting over a wealthy white man is good, then the media has done their job well. The programming is real.

You can see many of the influences placed on our children as soon as they start watching cartoons. One of the ways that we can combat this is to simply spend more time with our kids, limit the amount of TV that they consume daily. I understand that it is easier said than done but we must protect our youth. They are the future and we must plan and take action to make our future better as a collective.

Finding time is an issue for many parents especially single parent households. You will see some tips in the upcoming parts of this book as go into other parts of it. The media machine is always working to distract you.

Part 3 Education
Are the schools really teaching anything?

Another area to examine is the education system. You've got to remember the public schools are weapons of mass miseducation and they really don't educate in a beneficial way for our children. The school to prison pipeline a serious problem. They send your young boys to the slow classroom or the so called bad class for the bad kids. Many call them the bad eggs or the kids that don't want to listen.

Special education is what they call it to be politically correct. Pile them up in a room and put them on a computer to keep them quiet. In this setting they are separated from the "general population" of students just like convicts are separated in prisons across America.

They don't learn anything and then they push them along through each grade and before you know it, what are they doing? They are going straight into a life of crime. They never learned anything in school and now, the parents are at work 40+ hours a work-week so the parents are not really raising them and it's just a big cycle that never ends.

So I always tell people, if we are not reaching the kids what are we doing anything for? If we are not reaching the youth we are wasting our time on multiple levels. No matter what we do today to solve these problems, to combat this racism-white supremacy or any other issue, we are going to still be in the system locked in because the kids are being put right back into a failing school system.

Now some people may say, let's do homeschooling, that's an option but homeschooling is only as good as the people teaching it and if we were miseducated, how are we going to teach the kids knowledge of self?

So we have to dig into this and actually build our own schools and our own institutions, our own everything. We must create our own systems that can be copied from the public school system. There must be a complete overhaul of the curriculum that actually teach the skills that we need to survive in this capitalist society.

Part 4   Economics
Where is our economic base?

That brings me into the next area which is economics.

The area of economics is very important because this economic base will be used to solve all of our problems. We have to start and grow businesses that serve the needs of our communities. We must sell our culture to ourselves. It is as simple as that.

It's the only way to do it according to our black scholars like Dr. Boyce Watkins and Dr. Claud Anderson. Without an economic base we are forced into a system of low paying jobs and dependence on the government to feed us, clothe us, house us and everything else. That's why they have the black woman locked in the web as well.

Many black women feel like DWIGHT MAN is her baby daddy. He is putting her on, like a stupid video you might have seen on Facebook or social media a little while back with the dark skin chick with the blonde hair talking about, "thank you government for putting me on."   That is crazy! That's the mentality because they have programmed us to believe that the black woman doesn't need the black man and in reality, financially, she doesn't.

The government supports her with the food stamps, WIC, section 8 and much more. Is all of this government support really helping or hurting black people in this country? I don't know if that's all set up to help us or not. I think it's a hindrance. This government makes us way too dependent on the powers that be.

We have been taught that the love of money is the root to all evil. The fact of the matter is that the LACK of money is the root of all evil. No money increases crime and many other factors.

A few wealthy black people at the top is not the complete answer. Some even think that they are not the answer at all. You can have as much money as you want. What you do with that money is what makes the difference. Building infrastructure and establishing means of production and distribution is the answer to the economic problem.

In my opinion, entrepreneurship is the only way to economic freedom. Many have made it to super stardom like many of our great entertainers. The problem is that they really do not own anything and they are working to make others rich while they maintain control and rights to your music and more.

The late artist Prince understood this quite well and so did Michael Jackson and Sam Cooke of the 1960s. It seems like anyone who attempts to buck the system mysteriously dies at a younger age than expected. Without the distribution network, you still must be dependent on the powers that be to help you with producing films, television shows and like I mentioned above, your music.

The good news is the internet is changing all of that. This is the information age and there is really no excuse for ignorance anymore. You can easily become a graduate of YouTube University. Google knows just about everything. Put that together with live streaming video apps like periscope and you can learn any and everything straight from a person with experience from the other side of the world.

Part 5   Sex
How is sex being used to distract us?

The next area is sex. They are promoting sex on television with the entertainment and shows like Empire. Basically promoting this homosexual activity in the black community. It's the cool thing now, everybody is down and if you are not a bisexual woman, you are not in, you are not cool.

You may even hear men say, "I like girls, who like girls", which is one of the dumbest quotes out. If the girls like girls, that means less women to choose from on the market actually seeking to build a family.

There are many dudes in the closet acting like they don't like dudes but they like dudes. The bigger thing in now is crossdressing, trans-gendering or whatever you want to call it. The LGBT community is taking over the black empowerment movement.

From what I can see, black lives matter is nothing more than gay lives matter. That's what it's all about. And they have been promoting it from the very beginning and the very onset of when this started. Our civil rights struggle has basically been hijacked. Like Dr. Umar Johnson says, "You cannot equate the gay struggle with the black struggle."

That's just the real truth of the matter. People don't want to look at it for what it is, they have a catchy name, black lives matter, but two of the three people who started it were what? Homosexuals! You may live homosexuality lifestyle, but that's not a natural way of life. That is one of the major ways that they can stop black people from populating the earth or populating this country.

I was in the barber shop explaining this to an older black gentleman. I stated that black people naturally have a lot of babies and it is part of our

DNA. He said if I was white and made that remark then I would be considered racist. I told him that I am glad to be black!

His position was that we should not be having babies so much without an economic plan or money to raise that child. He also said that this teen pregnancy is way out of control. I explained how the natural order of our people is to have babies, a lot of babies and many times at a young age. The power structure understands that blacks have a lot of babies so that is why it is programmed into our minds that having children is so bad.

Prior to this capitalist society called America, we were having a lot of babies and there was no problem. Now that money is involved we seem to be caught between a rock and a hard place when it comes to having a lot of children.

When you look back into your own family, you may notice that grandma had 14-15 kids. Now just a few generations later 2 kids feel like too much for many people. That is all due to economics and the media showing us how bad it is to be a "teen mom" or have multiple children. Over population of Africans on the planet is a problem for the pale European. They have placed systems in place to attempt to keep the black population at a tolerable number.

It's serious, they've got the Planned Parenthood, making sure that the black babies have been aborted at alarming rates, killing millions of babies every year. You only see their offices in our communities. This is just one of the ways eugenics is alive and well in the hood.

From what I can see, homosexuality is the main weapon of choice against the black community at this time. There are some scholars in our community that talk about this topic all of the time. If you want to check out more information on the effects of this homosexual stuff check out Irritated Genie.

He drops the knowledge on the effects of homosexuality in our neighborhoods. He basically breaks it down telling you that if you are a person who plays chess, this is like a checkmate. It's one thing that black people have been double castrated, single castrated, beaten, burned alive and all these other stuff, right? Murdered, maimed, and burned alive right? That's one thing but as long as we have the black man with the black woman, making black babies, white-supremacy cannot win because there is another generation of black babies coming into the world to continue our cause.

They can't win if we continue making babies & building families. We are still in the game but once they program you and tell you that the woman doesn't like anyone but women and the man doesn't like anyone but men they've got a checkmate because you can't make babies now.

That's stopping the growth, like I said, coupled with Planned Parenthood, coupled with poverty and all the other stuff. It all comes together as forming population control or eugenics.

Racism-white supremacy is a system and it's not about an individual saying, "you are a no good nigger!" It's about the system as a whole. I never understood this coming up when I first heard it, I thought it was a joke, coming up back in the 90's and stuff. When people said it like, "the white man got his foot on my neck!" But I see what they are talking about now. When you actually do some study and take a look at it, you see exactly what's really going on and you'll see the truth.

The proof is in the pudding. What I'm saying is that the homosexuality lifestyle is running rampant in the black community, especially for a city like Atlanta, they say mostly everybody there is part of the rainbow flag coalition. Now states are passing laws against discrimination of people's sexual orientation and if you can be hired for a job or not. Not to mention the transgender restrooms and so much more is on the way.

IS IT POSSIBLE TO BE A BLACK REVOLUTIONARY WHILE THE WHITE MAN STILL CUTS YOUR PAYCHECK?

@ChrisMonroeSTL

Part 6   Labor
Do we need more jobs in our community?

This brings us to the next area which is labor.   Our community suffers from the highest unemployment rates and we are the lowest paid. The labor and employment brings us right back into economics. We must start our own businesses so we can employ our own people and not have to beg others for some job or beg somebody for opportunities to feed our families.
Back in the day we would say, "please boss, let me shine your shoes and wash your car." And things like "what's the matter boss, we sick." Malcolm X spoke on this type of slave mentality. The field negro vs. the house negro.

The reason we need more businesses is to control the flow of dollars within our communities. The black dollar leaves out of the black community in as little as 7 hours. If you do not believe this, I will ask you the following questions.

If you need food or groceries, who do you go see?
If you need gasoline for your vehicle, who do you go see?
Ladies, want to get your nails done? Who does them?
Your rent and mortgage payments go to who?
We all use toilet paper, who sells it to you?
The money you tithe to your church, where does it go?

Majority, if not ALL of the questions above had an answer of anyone but a black business. The answers are usually Arab, Caucasian, Oriental but notice the money leaves your community and goes straight to fund other races communities. We need that money to circulate within our communities before leaving to fund other ones. You may be thinking that your church money is not leaving your neighborhood, I will go into detail later in the religion part of this book.

Labor is one of those issues where you may hear people begging for raising the minimum wage. If you study the civil rights era of the 1960s, people are outright demanding jobs. Nobody needs to raise the minimum wage to pay you something that you are not worth. You've got to get your skill level up. Normally, if you are being paid minimum wage the reason is because your skill level isn't high enough. You may have to do some self-study to increase your knowledge base. Embrace the power of the internet with YouTube University and Google. You can learn almost anything today, there is no excuse for that.

So we must get the economics together so that we can hire our own people. Labor laws are written in their favor just like majority if not all of the other laws. These are simple things that black Americans can do for themselves. If we continue to sit on our hands and wait for someone to save us, we will be doomed. The time for action is NOW.

150 YEARS AGO WHEN SLAVERY WAS ABOLISHED, BLACKS OWNED 1/2 OF 1 PERCENT OF ALL OF THE WEALTH IN AMERICA.

@ChrisMonroeSTL
#iStayWoke

TODAY WITH ALL OF THE BLACK MILLIONAIRES & BILLIONAIRES, BLACKS *STILL* OWN *ONLY* 1/2 OF 1 PERCENT OF ALL OF THE WEALTH IN AMERICA.

Part 7   Law
Is the law on our side?

The next area is law. When you think about the law, what do you think about? The police terrorizing the black community? Exactly, and it goes even deeper than that. From the very founding fathers of this country when they wrote all the founding documents, black people were not included in that. Written in is three fifths of a man and much more. Many of the founding documents of the United States STILL have not been updated.

Pale Europeans came to America to make it perfect for them, NOT you. For example, you may hear the saying they were in search of life, liberty and the pursuit of <u>happiness</u> but that was never what they originally wrote. They wrote life, liberty and the pursuit of <u>property</u>. Guess who the property is that they were originally referring to?

African men, women, and children. The African, it's you they were referring to. YOU were the American dream.

So when the European forefathers came to The New World in the late 1400's they basically had it set up for them to prosper and for your African ancestors to work. Many Europeans can come here and get free land or a loan on some land and free labor by getting free slaves on a credit. So this capitalist society and the building of this country was all built from the very onset on the back of my African ancestors with FREE labor. Side note, black people were on ALL continents of this planet prior to the pale European.

A great book to read is called Black Labor, White Wealth by Dr. Claud Anderson. This book goes into detail explaining all of this in detail.

The laws were written in their favor back then and it still holds true today. You must know how the judicial, legislative, executive, local, state and federal government all work against black people as a system, not just name calling and empty threats. In my opinion, the legislative branch has never written a law that was really good for us. Even if it was written, it still must be enforced by the executive branch or when broken or interpreted by the judicial branch when there is a legal question. That means if all three branches of government are not on the same page, blacks still lose in the end. There is always a slick legal maneuver that keeps a lid on any uprising of consciousness.

Some may be asking, what about the civil rights laws?

Did the civil rights laws help us? Was being segregated better? You know, 50+ years of history would tell us the truth. I don't think it has really helped us. We put it in our minds that desegregation meant equality in America. Do you feel that things are equal?

We were better-off separated and that's the whole answer really to all the problems of black people. We are going to have to separate and build our own. That's the truth that people don't want to hear on that.

Another thing that many black people do not want to be honest about is the fact that everyone can't be a part of the new movement if one ever develops. There are a large number of black people that believe they are white. I will name Stacey Dash as a prime example but there are many others. You may hear people call them coons.

I understand that black people are loving and loyal people. There's nothing wrong with that but you must know white-supremacy and black power will never live side by side in harmony. Therefore, when people say we can build this community right here, in reality it really won't work. I don't have a lot of faith in that. There must be rules, boundaries and limitations within our communities. We must have our own security, police force, and army for a real separation to work.

I think we must separate because the law is written against African-Americans. They write the laws bad on the legislative part. Next, you get caught up with the executive branch with the police and the state. Finally, you go to court with the Judicial branch and get multiple years in prison. That is if the police don't kill you in cold blood on the street like Laquan McDonald, Eric Garner, Tamir Rice and countless others.

For example, let's say you've got a traffic violation. Think of all these little municipalities making all this money on speeding tickets or you got a tail light out, no auto insurance etc. They can lock you up and then if you can't afford the ticket you get more fines and pay more money. There are townships building big palaces and castles as police stations off of your back. They are basically buying everything like top notch police cars. You've seen the police cars they got with all this high tech equipment. The militarization of the police is a serious problem that should not be overlooked.

Who do you think pays for that? Ticket fines and taxpayers pay for a large amount of it. A lot of the revenue is generated from these traffic tickets. The laws are written against you and they will stack these fines up on you and if you don't have an economic base, or money you can never, ever, ever, get out of that hole.

The next thing you know; you have to pay for them hauling off your vehicle because they decided to tow your car. Don't forget you've got to get SR22 insurance and all this stuff comes back to the basics of no economics. We will suffer forever until we get the economic game together. That's why I promote entrepreneurship. That's what I talk about that all the time, start a business or invest in business. Dr. Boyce Watkins teaches that everyone should at least own a part of a business.

Entrepreneurship is the only way to economic freedom. It is just the answer that makes the most sense to me. As a bigger picture, black people as a whole are going to end up always having to separate. I don't think we can do it here in this country, it just seems impossible.

How can black people make up 13-14% of the US population but make up 51 percent of the prison population? How did that happen? Maybe Bill Clinton and Hillary Clinton of the 90's have something to do with that. The three strikes laws passed by the Clinton administration has taken a huge toll on the black community. There is no economic base that's why the crime is so high in our communities. That takes us right into the next topic which is war.

Part 8　　War
Warfare is real. Do we know who the enemy is?

There is definitely a war on the black man. We are being killed in the streets by each other and police. Now let's talk about this black on black crime myth. Yes, we kill each other but so does every other race, they kill each other as well but we do things at a higher rate simply because we don't have that economic base. When you don't have money, crime, drugs, prostitution and other low life things like that become rampant. It's just that simple.

We don't have enough businesses to employ our own people, which means we don't have jobs. No jobs mean no money and no money means a life of crime. It pushes many into a fight or flight mode. So what do you think the end result will be?

Many end up selling crack, breaking into cars, and many other crimes. The next thing you know; you have fallen victim to the streets or you fall right into the legal system that you can never get out of.

Once you get into the legal system you are locked into it and now you can't vote, you can't participate in anything because you have felonies on your record. So it becomes heads they win, tails you lose.

Many of the problems in our black communities are rooted in the breakup of the family. Add in the lack of an economic base and it makes a great recipe for failure. Getting your money up is just the first step. Then we MUST build means of production and distribution. The systems are what we lack, not just money. This is a capitalist society and if you have no money you have no voice. The police will always enforce the law, but if your pockets are full of lint balls only then you have lost already. Majority see you as the enemy as they saw Sandra Bland.

Many police officers see most black people as bad people due to the propaganda seen in the media and their own experience dealing with some of the worse people in society. So it's a police culture, they break it down and put on a tag on the black man and on black people as a whole. And that's why I say it is racism; white supremacy is a complete system. It goes much deeper than the words people use to hurt your feelings.

This system is setup to keep blacks locked in a box. When you get locked up by the police and that takes you right into the political system. Get slapped with a felony, now you cannot vote. Now you cannot even participate in the poli-tricks, not politics, poli-tricks, because they trick us every time we turn our heads. You look away they tell you one thing and do another.

Part 9   Politics AKA PoliTRICKS
Should black people participate in politics and voting?

When it comes to politics, we need elected leaders that will stand up for the black community instead of selling us out in a heartbeat for money. Politics is run by money. Dr. Claud Anderson breaks this down really good, and I've got the video on my YouTube channel @ChrisMonroeSTL

In the video he is showing you the entire step by step breakdown of how we get out of this wreck, and it's all based on economics. It is described as a five story building. The first floor is economics. You build up your businesses, you buy from each other, you sell your culture to each other, you build up money and you circulate that money within the community.

Once you get that money circulating you buy, rent or lease politicians in your precincts to operate on your behalf. Politicians respond mostly by money. Since black people don't have an economic base we have no real voting power. It's just that simple, we must practice group economics and group poli-tricks. You take the money from the economic base to buy your politicians. Once you have your politicians, then you move into the court legal system and the police.

After you have a way to influence those groups, you influence the police and the court system, move up and then you go into the media. For example, radio, newspapers, TV and all other types of media like that. You've got people like Rush Limbaugh who can bad mouth black people. You have no way to respond and combat the propaganda machine.

You are not able to communicate with your people because we don't own any TV or radio stations. The ones we do own such as Radio 1 with Cathy Hughes or TV1, look at their programming. What are they putting on the air all the time? Pure coonery, violence, overly sex driven content, you know stuff that's just not really helping black people.

They do a little bit here and there but overall they are just perpetuating everything that the mainstream media wants us to see and hear on a regular basis. You see and hear the worst of the worse. Black people showing you that the black woman is the angry black woman. The bad black man is doing criminal activities.

We have to paint a picture of ourselves in a positive light, not just negative all of the time. Positive images are what we need to see more of. Then after you get through the media portion then you go into the education. You bring up the youth with the same doctrine.

It is really that simple, economics to politics, politics to the court system and the police system, court system and the police system to the media, the media to inform your people and then all the way up to education. We have to build our institutions and teach our children these formulas to come up and just rinse and repeat, it's just that simple, rinse and repeat.

It may take years to perfect this simple solution. It will take some hard work and dedication, but I believe this is a good strategy all based in economics. We make it seem hard but it really is not that difficult. It's a simple plan that can be actually implemented today but we just don't want to do it.   We want to work for others. Sounds like a slave mentality, that post traumatic slavery syndrome like Dr. Joy Degruy talks about, the great mother teacher.

Blacks need to work as a group and not so much as individuals. We are voting straight ticket Democrat, thinking that the Democrats are going to save us. All they are doing is giving us little trinkets to pacify us to keep us on the bottom. Can't you see that? Democrats give you stuff to make you want to vote for them. The stuff they are giving you was yours in the first place. Power and control is what it's all about.

My mother told me vote straight ticket Democrat because they are for the people. That's what her mother told her. That's what my mothers, mothers, mother told her to do as well. Doing the same things over and over again while expecting different results. It sounds a lot like insanity to me.

The Republicans are really no better but we can't even do anything if we don't vote as a group with a platform, with actual things that are making a difference, we have to do that. Black people give their vote away for cheap. Our vote has very little power due to two main things.

First, as we should know by now, no economic base. Second is the simple fact that Democrats know that black will vote for them majority of the time no matter what. Republicans know that majority of black Americans will not vote for them. Historically, the GOP gets 8-10% of the black vote. Therefore, blacks have no voice because we are so predictable.

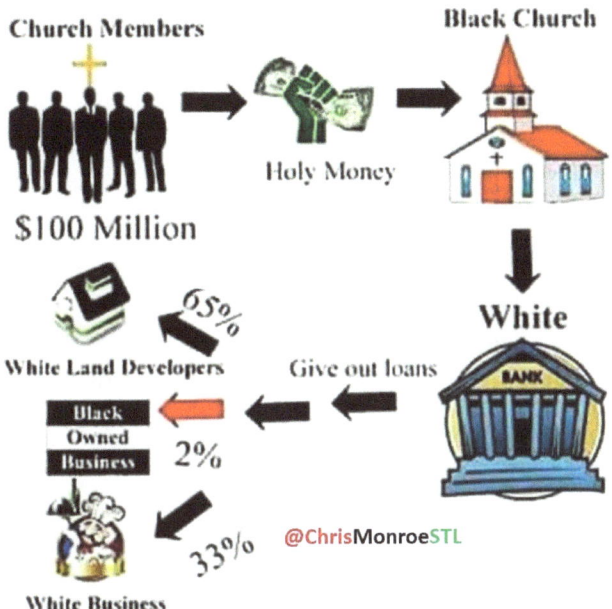

How Black Church dollars Flow

Church Members
$100 Million
Holy Money
Black Church
White
65%
White Land Developers
Give out loans
Black Owned Business
2%
33%
White Business
@ChrisMonroeSTL

Part 10   Religion
Where did all of these religions come from? Is it helping us?

This section may be difficult for you. You must know that I do not dislike any religion and people can worship and praise whoever they please. However, you must see the effects mentally and financially. Our people are sick and we have been told so many lies that no one knows what or who to believe.

There are three main points I would like to address when it comes to this topic. The economic part as well as history and origin. Black people seem to be the most religious people on the planet. Why is that? That means we should be the wealthiest or the most well off people on this planet. Has our holiness paid off in any real way for the masses of black people or has it just help fund our oppression?

We give on all our money to these churches and where does that money go? That money goes right into a white bank. The diagram above shows you how the money flows. The money leaves the black church to be deposited into a white bank that will NOT give you a loan. 2% of that money comes back to the black neighborhoods. The other 98% is used to make loans to white businesses and land developers. These same land developers could be the ones buying up the land in your neighborhood.

The economic issue is a real issue. Big mama worked her whole life and paid tithes to her church, just to find out in the end that the money she gave was the same money that put her out on the street when the land developers wanted to bulldoze her house to put in a strip mall.

What businesses do you see in the hood? Churches, liquor stores, Chinese shops are the majority. Every one of those take money right out of our neighborhoods to build up other communities and not ours. We have a parasite sucking the life out of our communities economically. Some studies say that black spent over 1 trillion dollars last year.
Where did all of this money go? Into everybody else's pockets! Follow the money to find the real answers. Numbers don't lie right?

It seems like one of those things that's just never going to change. We are going to keep funding our own oppression, doing the same thing over and over and over expecting different results. That makes no sense! How can we continue to do the same thing expecting different results?

One of the biggest issues that I can see is that black people operate in emotions way too much. I can understand that many of us may be looking for love, but we still must remain smart. We base too many decisions on feelings. We truly want to do the right thing at heart. The problem is that others will take complete advantage of you. They use our love for Jesus to use it as the most effective weapon against our people.

It's a serious problem when you look at the numbers. We are not operating on numbers and logic; we are stuck in our emotions. What are you going to do with 2 percent of money that you sent to the bank when you should be using that money to circulate within your own community? That's the part that we must see. It makes no sense to continue to keep doing this.

Creflo Dollar is getting a $65 Million jet, you've got TD Jakes and all of these others that are clean as a whistle. Look at the cars and stuff they are buying? They are doing extremely well. They are getting paid and white-supremacy is getting paid, we are funding our own oppression.

Next, I will just touch on the history versus HIS story when it comes to religion. As far as history, you will find if you did even a light amount of study that the bible is full of plagiarism. Let's start there with the bible. Many black Americans read and study the King James Version of the bible.

Who was King James? He was a homosexual king of England that sanctioned a new updated version of the bible starting in 1604 and completed in 1611. It saddens me that black people can base their entire life off of something from only 400 years ago. Who authorized King James to change the word of God? If he can change the bible, could the pope change it today? Could the president of the United States change the bible and make a 2017 version? Why not? Just a few basic questions to ask.

If you study the holy trinity story of the father, son and the holy spirit I would like to ask you where is the female in the story? Every human you have every met in your life came from a woman. This story was stolen from Kemet, better known as Egypt today. The real story is still on the walls waiting on you to read it. Below is the cast of character break down. Click the link for the full story.

The Story of **Ausar** (Osiris), **Au set** (Isis), and **Heru** (Horus)

Biblical Name	Father/God	Son/Jesus	Mother/Mary
Greek	Osirus	Horus	Isis
Original Name	Auset	Heru	Ausar

The bible in general is pro slavery, anti-woman and anti-African. When I say anti-African, I am referring to the anti-Egyptian words. How bad is pharaoh in the bible? I am not saying that all of the teachings are bad but I will give you a few scriptures that you should review to verify the statements I have made.

Ephesians 6:5 Slaves, obey your earthly masters with respect and fear, and with sincerity of heart, just as you would obey Christ.

1 Peter 2:18 Slaves, in reverent fear of God submit yourselves to your masters, not only to those who are good and considerate, but also to those who are harsh.

1 Timothy 6:1 All who are under the yoke of slavery should regard their masters as fully worthy of honor, so that God's name and our teaching will not be discredited.

1 Timothy 2:11 Let the woman learn in silence with all subjection.

Luke 12:47 And that servant, which knew his lord's will, and prepared not *himself*, neither did according to his will, shall be beaten with many *stripes*.

Exodus 21:20-21 20"If a man strikes his male or female slave with a rod and he dies at his hand, he shall be punished.21"If, however, he survives a day or two, no vengeance shall be taken; for he is his property.

Above are just a few of the scriptures you never hear in church. I have about 25 others that you should investigate. Also, while conducting any type of research you may find that 8 out of the 10 commandments were stolen. They come from the 42 laws of Ma 'at in Kemet. Just about every story in the bible was made up or stolen from a religion prior to it. I go on and on about the lies, and plagiarism in the bible but I think you get my drift. This is not about a belief, I am going off of facts and evidence.

Remember that we are in the information age and there is no excuse for ignorance anymore. If you want to keep your belief, that is up to you. I just want you to know that there are answers to your questions. I just wanted to drop a few nuggets in this book but there is so much more that your mind would be blown.

As I said above, none of these points are made to attack your particular religion. This is just some basic information you should be aware of. The major three monotheistic religions are Judaism, Christianity and Islam in that order. According to Dr. Yosef Alfredo Antonio Ben-Jochannan better known as "Dr. Ben" who is a scholar in African history, there are many loopholes and lies in all three religions.

According to the bible Abraham is the first Jew. His mother or father were not of the Hebrew faith. Abraham was supposedly born in 1685 B.C.E.

B.C. = Before Christ
B.C.E. = Before Common Era
A.D. = After Death
C.E. = Common Era

Judaism was first, then came Christianity, finally there was Islam. These three religions have a grandparent, parent, child relationship. They are ALL man made. Some say that they are crowd control for the masses of people on the earth. It just effects black people more because of simple programming.

The first time a black person heard the name Jesus was on a slave ship. The good ship Jesus was the name of one of the first slave ships bringing kidnapped Africans to the new world.

One more basic point is that the letter "J" is approximately 500 years old. How could someone named Jesus exist without that very important letter? I could go into a lot more details on religion but I think you understand that these religions are tools used for white-supremacy to conquer the world. When Europeans colonized Africa, the people had the land and the European had the bible. They said, let us pray. When the Africans eyes had reopened, the Europeans had the land and the Africans had the bible. That's not a fair exchange is it?

IF T.D. JAKES WROTE AND RELEASED A NEW BIBLE NEXT YEAR.

@ChrisMonroeSTL

#iStayWoke

WOULD YOU GET RID OF THE KING JAMES VERSION OF THE BIBLE...?

Conclusion

All of those points I've been talking about are things we must become fully aware of. These are places we must combat on multiple levels and know that systematic racism is real. This has nothing to do with hating or loving pale Europeans. These are principles and areas that we are being attacked at on a daily basis.

The areas of battle are entertainment, education, economics, sex, labor, law, war, politics and religion. Religion is the one that's doing an incredible amount of damage psychologically. The book tells us to love our enemy, embrace our oppressors and be a good slave. Many people will think, no that's not right, but I love Jesus. While you are sitting up here trying to wait to go see Jesus when you die and so called go to heaven, you have got the white man, the Arab man, the East Indian and everybody else building their heaven in your hood, not your neighborhood, in your hood.

All of the areas covered play an intricate part in global racism white-supremacy. Each area plays an important role to keep the black power struggle muted and reduced as much as possible. Here are some basic things to remember.

-Keep the black man and woman against each other in every way.
-Make sure the black family structure remains broken.
-Continue to miseducate and program the next generation to continue their mission, not ours.
-Keep us voting straight ticket Democrat without question.
-Maintain economic power and control of our dollars
-Emotionally connect with us through religion
-Homosexuality is a form of eugenics (population control)

They are building their heaven in your hood with your money and you don't even see it. So we got to wake up people, we have got to wake up. This stuff goes deeper than this, I just wanted to give a basic overview on these topics.

People you MUST know about

Below you will find a list of names that you must know about. There are many heavy hitters in the black conscious movement. I believe these people can give you a better understanding of the problems in the black community as well as give you some solutions. I do not agree with all positions taken by these people but I know that you can get a better degree of understanding from them.

Ashra Kwesi
Brother Polight
Dr. John Henrik Clark
(Dr. Ben) Yosef Alfredo Antonio Ben-Jochannan
Dr. Boyce Watkins
Dr. Umar Johnson
Dr. Ray Hagins
Dr. Claud Anderson
Dr. Joy Degruy
Dr. Frances Cress Wesling
Dr. Sebi
David Banner
Irritated Genie
Mfundishi Jhutym
Michelle Alexander
Professor Griff

There are many others that cover the topics in this book. This small group of scholars can definitely help you during your transition from asleep to being awake. I am Mr. I Stay Woke!

Thank you for reading. Please remember to leave a review of this book and share with friends or family. "I will see you, before you see me!"

Social Media Connections - Connect online with Chris Monroe

Main Website – CHRISMONROESTL.COM

Facebook Personal Profile – facebook.com/chrismonroestl

Facebook Like Page – facebook.com/istaywokeblackpower

PeriScope – periscope.tv/chrismonroestl

YouTube - @ChrisMonroeSTL

Twitter - @ChrisMonroeSTL

InstaGram - @ChrisMonroeSTL

LinkedIN - @ChrisMonroeSTL

SnapChat - @ChrisMonroeSTL

Anchor FM - @ChrisMonroeSTL

For speaking engagements, wholesale orders and any other special request you may send an email to **contact@chrismonroestl.com**

Special Thanks to:

Sage Merritt

Rose & Robert Harmon

Matthew Robinson

Special thanks to my periscope family

@SageSpeaks, @DLeeInspires, @The_Vessel, @Ms_Cotton,
@MissAllisonKirk, @MoniqMills, @Heavylover, @primetime7pm09,
@izzy420high, @KCbizBOSS, @JazzyJuJuBee, @AshaTyson,
@GaryVee, @LizaBitty, @Himay10nence, @AshleyAnnEvent,
@TheRealKQuick, @AkaShawnThomas and the thousands of others who
watch, follow and connect daily. You are appreciated.

CHRISMONROESTL.COM